# Cape Cod

## Martha's Vineyard & Nantucket

A PHOTOGRAPHIC PORTRAIT

PHOTOGRAPHY BY

**Paul Scharff**

NARRATIVE BY

**Karen T. Bartlett**

First published in the United States of
America by:

Twin Lights Publishers, Inc.
8 Hale Street
Rockport, Massachusetts 01966
Telephone: (978) 546-7398
http://www.twinlightspub.com

ISBN: 1-885435-83-5
ISBN: 978-1-885435-83-5


10 9 8 7 6 5 4 3 2 1

**Waiting it Out** *(opposite)*
FIRST ENCOUNTER BEACH, EASTHAM

Powerful receding tides along the coast
of Cape Cod can expose a mile or more
of ocean bottom, leaving sculpted sand
formations, sparkling ribbons of shallow
water, and an occasional boat.

*(frontispiece)*
LECOUNT HOLLOW BEACH, WELLFLEET

*(jacket front)*
HOWES BEACH, DENNIS

*(jacket back)*
APTUCXET TRADING POST, BOURNE

Narrative by Karen T. Bartlett
www.karentbartlett.com
A former resident of New England,
Bartlett is an award-winning travel writer
whose work appears in books, magazines
and newspapers throughout North
America and the Caribbean.

Special thanks to Debra and Ken Traugot,
innkeepers/owners of the Beechwood Inn;
to Stephanie and John Lowell, owners of
East Dennis Oyster Farm; and to William
DeSousa-Mauk, Vice President of Michael
Patrick Communications, for going above
and beyond to help in our quest for accu-
racy and timeliness in the preparation of
this book.


Book design by:
SYP Design & Production, Inc.
www.sypdesign.com


Printed in China

# " ...you're sure to fall in love with old Cape Cod. "

The historic seaside communities of Cape Cod, Martha's Vineyard, and Nantucket stir the souls of artists and photographers, romantics, and scholars. A skyline of lighthouses, windmills and church spires, accented with a kaleidoscope of colorful wooden boats and rainbow-hued lobster buoys, are set against land and seascapes of tranquil ponds, raging surf, and heather-covered moors. Parabolic dunes that rise 80 to 100 feet inspire breathtaking awe.

Abundant wildlife draws bird-watchers and naturalists, while sports enthusiasts come for unparalleled sailing, fishing, kayaking, and kiteboarding. While cars may often be necessary for some ventures, the most delightful ways to experience Cape Cod, Martha's Vineyard and Nantucket are on foot, by bicycle, and by boat. There are more than 100 miles of dedicated bicycle paths, endless miles of winding country lanes, and pristine wooded and seaside trails.

There are sleepy villages and gentrified towns; vintage railroads and historic bridges; salty fishing wharves and fashionable yacht harbors. With architecture ranging from sea captains' mansions to quintessential seaside cottages including an entire village of Victorian Gingerbread houses—Cape Cod, Martha's Vineyard, and Nantucket are the stuff of artists' dreams.

Few beaches on earth compare with the forty unbroken miles of windswept seashore on Cape Cod, immortalized in Henry David Thoreau's 1865 book, *Cape Cod*. The dramatic, multi-hued mineral cliffs of Martha's Vineyard lure geologists to explore their mysteries. Centuries of powerful tides and violent nor'easters have created one of the largest shipwreck graveyards on the Atlantic Coast, including Black Sam Bellamy's pirate ship that went down in 1717.

From historic Sandwich at Cape Cod's upper arm, to its oyster-rich elbow, to the vibrant and colorful art colony of Provincetown at its fist, the Cape encompasses 413 square miles. Martha's Vineyard covers 100 square miles, and tiny Nantucket—once the whaling capital of the world—is tucked into just 50 square miles. Throughout the 563 square-mile maritime landscape are hundreds of fine art galleries, artisans studios and craft boutiques. A striking, 252-foot high monument celebrates the fact that it was the tip of Cape Cod, not Plymouth, where the Mayflower first landed.

Local museums are rich with treasures, from quahog-shell wampum to pirate pieces of eight; from Mayflower Pilgrim-related artifacts to treasures from the heyday of whaling. A wealth of 17th to 20th century collections range from the bells of town criers to John F. Kennedy's personal family photos.

The Cape is the home of Peter Cottontail and Sandwich Glass. It was here, at America's oldest professional summer theater, that legendary stars like Bette Davis, Humphrey Bogart, and Gregory Peck made their stage debuts, and famed playwrights, the likes of Eugene O'Neill and Tennessee Williams, wrote and saw some of their first plays produced.

Whether you come to research the deepest secrets of the ocean, celebrate the ancestry of America, or experience the endless beauty of it all; whether you live here, or simply come for a steaming bowl of clam chowder and a taste of the most succulent oysters in the world, may Paul Scharff's evocative photography on these pages keep the memories fresh, and bring you back again.

**Brant Point Light** (*opposite*)
NANTUCKET

Near the Nantucket ferry landing, standing just 26 feet tall, Brant Point Light occupies the site of the second lighthouse built in America, 30 years after Boston Light. Though destroyed many times by fire and wind, the spirit of the original remains intact.

### Bourne Bridge

BOURNE

Along with her look-alike, the Sagamore Bridge over the Cape Cod Canal, the historic cantilever Bourne Bridge opened in 1935 connecting the Cape with the mainland. Each bridge has a ship clearance of 135 feet.

**Cape Cod Canal** *(above)*
BOURNE

Part of the Intracoastal Waterway, the approximately 17 mile-long man-made Cape Cod Canal connects Cape Cod Bay to Buzzards Bay. The widest sea level canal in the world, it is spanned by two highway bridges and a railroad bridge.

**Sagamore Bridge** *(opposite, top)*
BOURNE

When it was built, the 616-foot horizontal span of the Sagamore Bridge made it the longest list span in the world. It brings as many as 200,000 vehicles on a single summertime weekend over Buzzard's Bay from U.S. Route 6.

**Railroad Bridge** *(opposite, bottom)*
BOURNE

The Railroad Bridge, supported by 271-foot high towers, is the second longest lift bridge in the U.S. Though there is no longer train service from the mainland, the Cape Cod Central Railroad still uses it for sightseeing and dinner excursions.

**Jonathan Bourne Historical Center** *(top)*
BOURNE

When it split from Sandwich in 1884, Bourne became Cape Cod's second town. Many of its buildings and artifacts date back to the 1600s. This library-turned museum was named for one of the founding fathers, whaling ship owner, Jonathan Bourne.

**Walking Tour** *(bottom)*
BOURNE

The Bourne Center is an ideal starting point to tour some of the oldest historic sites on Cape Cod, including the Briggs-McDermott House, a fine example of early 19th Century Greek Revival architecture with period furnishings.

**Recycled Windmill** *(opposite)*
BOURNE

Joseph Jefferson, the Cape Cod actor who portrayed Rip Van Winkle, used this Dutch-style windmill as an art studio back in the time of his good friend President Grover Cleveland, who had a summer home here. Relocated to the Aptucxet Museum complex, it's now a gift shop.

**Trading with Wampum**

BOURNE

The original Aptucxet Trading Post was built in 1627 by the Plymouth Colony. Its excavated foundation may be the earliest remains of a Pilgrim building. The Pilgrims used wampum, the currency made from local quahog shells, to trade with the Indians.

**Aptucxet Museum**

BOURNE

The museum collection includes arrowheads, wampum, and other period artifacts. Most mysterious is the Bournedale Stone. Some say it is a rune stone dating back to the Viking era. The museum offers history tours and classes in basket making and wampum bead making.

## Glass Art

SANDWICH

Mason jars catch the light at the Green
Briar Nature Center. In the 1900s, they
may have held homemade strawberry
rhubarb jam or plum chutney from Ida
Putnam's Jam Kitchen. The Thornton W.
Burgess Society offers demonstrations
and classes in the historic Jam Kitchen.

**Green Briar Nature Center** *(top and bottom)*
SANDWICH

Beloved Cape Cod storybook author
Thornton W. Burgess would have appreciated this whimsical sign on the lawn
at The Green Briar Nature Center.
The famous Briar Patch, home of Peter
Cottontail, has nature trails through real
briar thickets just like in the stories.

**Rainbow over Shawme Lake** *(top)*
SANDWICH

The beautiful spire of the First Church of Christ, the turning of the leaves, and a perfect rainbow over Shawme Lake cast an enchanting aura over an early autumn morning in Sandwich.

**Solitary Moment** *(bottom)*
SANDWICH

Resident swans share their sanctuary with a lone fisherman on Shawme Lake. The lake is a kettle pond, which is a body of fresh water created more than 18,000 years ago from glacial depressions. There are more than 350 kettle ponds on Cape Cod.

### The Golden Hour

SANDWICH

Incorporated in 1639, the historic seaside community of Sandwich was the first town on Cape Cod and is one of the oldest towns in the United States. Its many period homes are especially lovely when the leaves turn red and gold.

**17th-Century Grist Mill** *(top and bottom)*
SANDWICH

Fresh ground corn is still available in
season at Dexter's Grist Mill on Shawme
Lake. Historic features of this circa 1654
working grist mill in Sandwich include
ancient stone walls and the
original millstone.

## Scenic Boardwalk

SANDWICH

Traversing more than 1,000 feet of marshes, rivers, and dunes, the Sandwich Boardwalk commands awe-inspiring views. In 1991, Hurricane Bob destroyed it, and residents sold more than 2,000 planks to raise money for rebuilding. Names and sentiments are engraved on the planks.

## Sandwich Glass Museum

SANDWICH

Sandwich Glass of the 1800s-era is prized the world over. The factory in Sandwich was created by Deming Jarves, who perfected the machine that produces its most famous product. Jarves and his artisans also made blown, cut, and molded glass. The Sandwich Glass Museum turned 100 in 2007. It now has more than 5,000 pieces on display in 15 galleries, and offers demonstrations in the glass art.

## Thornton W. Burgess Museum
SANDWICH

Thornton W. Burgess, creator of the beloved character, Peter Cottontail, is honored in his hometown of Sandwich. Burgess wrote some 15,000 syndicated newspaper stories and 170 children's books. The grounds have an award-winning herb garden and wildflower garden.

**Research at Work**

WOODS HOLE

Woods Hole revolves around a scientific community, yet retains the distinctive flavor of Old Cape Cod. Organizations headquartered here include the Woods Hole Oceanographic Institution, the Marine Biological Laboratory, and NOAA's Northeast Fisheries Science Center.

**Town Center Stroll** *(top)*
WOODS HOLE

Woods Hole is hardly just a destination for oceanography buffs. The village and its surrounding region also please nature lovers and epicures; and shoppers delight in the unique blend of stores and galleries along the waterfront.

**Ship Ahoy** *(bottom)*
WOODS HOLE

Art, architecture, and nautical themes merge on Water Street, as illustrated by the landmark sculpture protruding from the wall of the Candle House. Built in the 1800s to store whale oil and make spermaceti candles, it now is used by the Marine Biological Laboratory.

## Woods Hole Oceanographic Institution
WOODS HOLE

WHOI (pronounced hoo-eee) is the largest private, nonprofit marine research organization in the world. Its mission is to conduct research to advance and communicate an understanding of the ocean's interaction with the Earth. Its focus includes natural hazards, ships and technology, climate change, global warming, and polar research. WHOI works with universities worldwide, from undergraduate to post-doctoral studies. It utilizes state-of-the-art instrumentation, including deep submergence vehicles and robotic seafloor mapping systems.

## U.S. Coast Guard

WOODS HOLE

The U.S. Coast Guard Sector Southeastern New England is one of the largest in the United States, with nearly 2,000 personnel, serving in multiple stations including a LORAN (Long Range Aids-to-Navigation Station).

**Native Cranberries** *(top)*
FALMOUTH

Peat bogs in Falmouth go red with cranberries in October when the waterlogged cranberries are ready for harvesting. The native Cape Cod fruit was said to be part of the Pilgrims first Thanksgiving feast.

**Watchful Gull** *(bottom)*
FALMOUTH

Food, and the art of acquiring it, is the raison d'etre for most species of gulls. Unable to crack tough oyster and clam shells, they drop them onto rocks and then swoop down to scoop out the bounty.

**Beach House** *(opposite)*
FALMOUTH

Window boxes of red geraniums or other vibrant flowers often provide the only spot of color in a typical Cape Cod scene. Unlike many summer cottages, an occasional beach house does have the comforts of a year-round residence.

**Historic Falmouth Village** *(top and bottom)*
FALMOUTH

To walk through Falmouth is to enter the pages of an artfully illustrated history book. There are shops to explore and a cemetery bearing names and dates from 1735. The Museums on the Green, consisting of two restored 18th-century homes, feature exhibits on whaling and maritime history and life of the period, including a re-created early 1800s doctor's office. Pictured is the memorial to the Falmouth veterans of World War I and the Spanish-American War.

**Tidal Pond**

FALMOUTH

After their first seaside homes succumbed to storms and erosion, early Cape Codders moved to sheltered waters inland from the coast. The combined salt and fresh water ecosystems of tidal ponds support a rich wildlife population.

**Falmouth Heights Beach** (*top*)
FALMOUTH

The graceful crescent of Falmouth
Heights Beach is popular with walkers,
and its shallow inlets make natural
splash pools for children.

**Ferries and Cruises** (*bottom*)
FALMOUTH

Besides basic transportation between
the Cape, Martha's Vineyard, and Nantucket there are harbor cruises, canal
cruises, lighthouse-viewing cruises, wine
and beer-tasting cruises, and excursions
to the Elizabeth Islands.

**A Schooner Moment**

NANTUCKET SOUND

There may not be a sweeter sight on a summer day than a three-masted schooner under full sail, gliding into view as it makes its fleeting pass between two golden dunes.

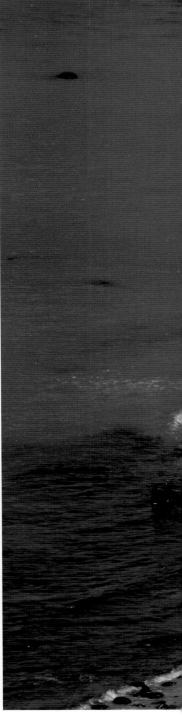

**Gay Head Light** (top)
MARTHA'S VINEYARD

High atop the 130-foot-high Aquinnah Cliffs (Gay Head) of Martha's Vineyard, the picturesque 1799 Gay Head Light presides over some of the most treacherous waters on the New England coast. It is open to the public on weekend evenings for sunset tours in summer.

**Nobska Point Light** (bottom)
MARTHA'S VINEYARD

Nobska Point lighthouse at Woods Hole is a favorite photo subject from the decks of passing boats. The grounds are open to the public and the lighthouse opens for scheduled tours. The Keeper's House is home to the commander of the Coast Guard sector that manages the station.

### Cliffs of Gay Head
MARTHA'S VINEYARD

For two centuries, artists have been captivated by the play of light on the multi-colored clay cliffs of Gay Head on the western shore of Martha's Vineyard. The beaches are public; the cliffs themselves, a National Landmark, are off limits for erosion control.

**Mineral Art**

MARTHA'S VINEYARD

Interactions of iron oxide with silts and sediments, silicate and clay minerals, with highlights of quartz and charcoal, create the paint-box hues of the Gay Head Cliffs. The unique mineral composition lures geologists from around the world.

**East Chop Light** *(top and right)*
MARTHA'S VINEYARD

Once called the Chocolate Lighthouse for its original brown color, the solitary cast iron 1878 lighthouse stands sentry 40 feet atop Telegraph Hill at the "chop," or entrance, to Vineyard Haven Harbor. It mirrors its Tisbury sibling, the West Chop Light.

**Menemsha Harbor** *(top)*
MARTHA'S VINEYARD

The historic Martha's Vineyard fishing village of Menemsha, with its scenic harbor, is a prime destination for fishermen and boaters. It also is a starting point for sightseeing charters and cycling excursions.

**Victoria Gazebo** *(left)*
MARTHA'S VINEYARD

Ocean Park, in Oak Bluffs, is surrounded by fashionable Victorian, Queen Anne, and Gothic Revival homes. The Victorian gazebo makes an artful backdrop for summer concerts and fireworks displays.

**Serenity on Menemsha Pond**
MARTHA'S VINEYARD

There are many tranquil moments on Menemsha Pond. At other times, sailors and paddlers thrive on the excitement of strong incoming tides and stiff breezes, especially at the north end of the pond.

**Along Tisbury Road**
MARTHA'S VINEYARD

Picket fences, gabled cottages swathed
in sun-washed gray cedar shake siding,
and profusions of summer flowers define
the inviting island nature of Martha's
Vineyard.

**Winding Roads** *(top)*
MARTHA'S VINEYARD

Pastoral country roads connect the hamlets, villages, and towns of Martha's Vineyard. From early spring to late fall, explorers may encounter sunflower fields, flower stalls, fruit and vegetable stands, and quaint shops that offer locally produced jams, jellies, and crafts.

**Dune Cottages** *(bottom)*
MARTHA'S VINEYARD

Sprinkled all along the coastline, just inland of the dunes, are quaint summer houses. Very few have manicured gardens; most reflect the true ambience of the Vineyard, surrounded by natural vegetation and kitchen gardens.

**Fashionable Edgartown** *(left)*
MARTHA'S VINEYARD

Stately 19th-century sea captains' mansions blend artfully with interesting shops and galleries, antique stores, museums, and eateries along the narrow streets of Edgartown, Martha's Vineyard, which overlooks one of America's finest yacht harbors.

**Black Dog Tavern** *(right, top and bottom)*
MARTHA'S VINEYARD

Clam chowder aficionados must not miss the opportunity to savor what some deem to be the best *chow-dah* in New England. The Black Dog Tavern, just west of Vineyard Haven center, is hard to miss, with its vintage 1914 rail car and the black dog presiding over the door. Ferry riders make the adjacent bakery their last stop before heading back across the harbor.

**At Anchor**

MARTHA'S VINEYARD

Look for any body of water around the Vineyard and you're sure to spot a fishing boat, sailboat, kayak, or canoe at rest. It's what they do here. This one was last seen bobbing peacefully at Hartsville Inlet.

### Cruising to the Vineyard
MARTHA'S VINEYARD

High-speed transport to Martha's Vineyard includes first-class charters, with comfortable inside as well as deck seating to catch the breezes and views. A trip between Falmouth and Oak Bluffs (Martha's Vineyard) takes 35 to 55 minutes, depending on speed and vessel.

**Sunrise at West Chop Light**

MARTHA'S VINEYARD

From its humble beginnings as a 25-foot rubblestone structure, the pristine white lighthouse with its pretty, red-roofed keeper's house has served mariners for nearly two centuries. The active Coast Guard station, closed to the public, is visible from West Chop Road.

**Edgartown Light** *(opposite)*

MARTHA'S VINEYARD

Originally built on pilings in the harbor, Edgartown Light eventually became landlocked by shifting sands. Legend says it was a favorite spot for one last kiss before whalers went out to sea, earning its nickname "Bridge of Sighs."

**Beach Roses** *(above)*

MARTHA'S VINEYARD

A rainbow palette of blues, greens, yellows, and pinks along Oak Bluff Road compels travelers to stop and smell the beach roses. Similar views are common throughout Martha's Vineyard.

**Vineyard Sound Harbor**

NANTUCKET

When the fish aren't biting, one can always pull up a chair and enjoy the view. These particular chairs, patiently awaiting their owners, overlook Vineyard Sound Harbor on Martha's Vineyard.

**Chowder, Lobsters, and Ambience** *(top)*
NANTUCKET

The Straight Wharf Fish Store on Nantucket gives the Vineyard's Black Dog Tavern a bit of friendly competition with its own homemade clam chowder. Chowder and lobster taste better when enjoyed on the harborfront dock.

**Number Two Old South Wharf** *(bottom)*
NANTUCKET

The gallery of popular sculptor David Hostetler is one of many treasures awaiting discovery in the weathered gray and white fish houses along the wharf. Nantucket is a thriving artist's haven with nearly 50 galleries and dozens more artisans' home studios.

### Bicycling the Island (*above*)
NANTUCKET

For a true Nantucket experience, one must slip down back roads and travel beside the crests of cliffs and dunes. The best views are often enjoyed from the seat of a bicycle. Cycling is the primary way locals get around their island.

### Window Boxes (*left*)
NANTUCKET

The question is not whether to have a window box, but what to plant in it. Boxes, baskets, pots, and even old boats, spill over with flowers from May to October.

### Another Dawn in Paradise
NANTUCKET

The silent salt air and the gentle slap of waves early on a Nantucket morning give no hint of the bustle of activity to come. Artists frequently set up their easels to capture such moments in oils, chalks, watercolors, and pastels.

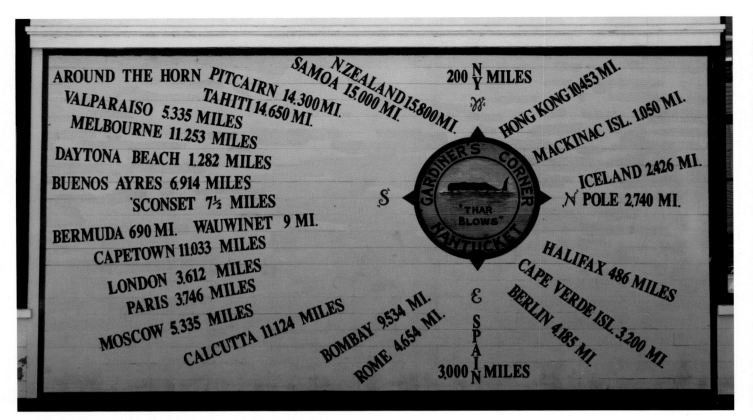

**Going Somewhere?** *(above)*
NANTUCKET

Some folks would wonder why you'd want to, if you're standing here at Gardiner's Corner in Nantucket Town; but here are the coordinates, just in case.

**Cobblestones** *(left)*
NANTUCKET

Big sailing ships needed ballast for stabilization, and England had plenty of big stones to spare. Once the ships were unloaded on Nantucket, the irregular shaped and earth-hued stones were laid out as a track for heavy horse carts.

## Meet Me at the Hub

NANTUCKET

"Meet me at the Hub" is a common phrase among Nantucket visitors, who love the tree-shaded benches, wide gas-lit cobblestone streets, brick sidewalks, and 19th century buildings-turned-boutiques in the center of town.

**Stunning Sunsets** *(top)*
BARNSTABLE

Like snowflakes, no two sunsets are alike. The brilliant lavender, red, or orange afterglow of a summer sunset often is even more spectacular than the sunset itself.

**Sandy Neck Light** *(bottom)*
BARNSTABLE

Since 1931, when its beacon was deactivated, the lighthouse in Barnstable Harbor has been of no help to lost mariners. It stood headless for 75 years until October 2007, when, to great fanfare and fireworks, the light was restored. The lighthouse is privately owned.

**Stage Island** *(opposite)*
BARNSTABLE

Luxury living combined with a front row seat at Mother Nature's theater defines life on Stage Island. Just five feet above sea level, the island overlooks salt marsh and the Bass River.

**Long and Winding Roads** *(opposite)*
CAPE COD

The first rule of thumb when exploring this region is simple: get off the beaten path. People who follow the back roads, while respecting private property, are rewarded with visual pleasures that highway travelers miss.

**Landscaping with Boats** *(above)*
BARNSTABLE

Nearly everyone in these parts either has a boat or access to one. When its nautical days come to an end, many a small boat finds new life as a landscaping accent for a park or a summer cottage.

### For Grownups Too

MASHPEE

The Cape Cod Children's Museum in Mashpee is just plain fun, with a pirate ship, a rowboat, and a train to climb aboard, as well as a planetarium, a puppet theater, a toddler play area, and family-friendly interactive exhibits.

## Centerville Historical Museum

CENTERVILLE

Tucked inside this 1840 house are a maritime gallery, a 19th-century schoolroom and a Colonial Revival kitchen, as well as artifacts, uniforms, and toys reflecting the history of Centerville. The gift shop carries unique collectibles from antique sailors' Valentine pins to local crafts.

**Wind Power** *(top)*
HYANNIS

Special fencing protects the fragile sands
of Kalmus Beach against erosion due to
powerful summer thermal winds. Those
same winds make Kalmus Beach a para-
dise for windsurfing and kitesurfing.
Facilities include a picnic area, conces-
sions, showers, and a lifeguard station.

**Aunt Betty's Pond** *(bottom)*
HYANNIS

Little is known about Aunt Betty except
that in the 1800s she had an apple
orchard bordering her namesake pond.
Cape Cod was named for a fish, and it's
unclear whether the name Martha's Vineyard honors founder Bartholomew
Grosnold's daughter or his mother-in-law.

**Sunrise Over Hyannis**

HYANNIS

Gold-infused sea grasses and a pink-tinged dawn sky greet early risers on Hyannis beaches. At this hour, the sand is still pleasantly cool, and the only foot-prints are those of the egrets and gulls. This wooden bridge at Colonial Way is one of many in Hyannis.

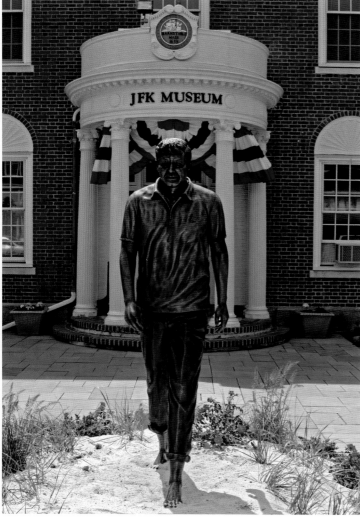

**John F. Kennedy Memorial** *(above)*
HYANNIS

A bronze medallion featuring the profile of beloved Hyannis citizen, and 35th U.S. President John F. Kennedy is imbedded in a stone wall facing Lewis Bay. The wall overlooks a small park with a fountain and benches.

**JFK Museum** *(left)*
HYANNIS

A life-size bronze statue by sculptor David Lewis depicts JFK walking barefoot, as he was remembered, along the beach in Hyannis Port. The museum's video gallery, hosted by Walter Cronkite, features hundreds of photographs of the 35th president's time on Cape Cod.

## Hyannis Harbor

HYANNIS

Stately yachts, weathered fishing boats, and ferry boats share the busy Hyannis Harbor, where picturesque wharfside restaurants are gathering places for boaters, land tourists, and locals. The harbor is walking distance to the JFK Museum, shops, and the train depot.

**Cape Cod Central Railroad** *(top and bottom)*

HYANNIS

All aboard the shiny red train at the
Hyannis Depot for a ride into the 1840s.
Passengers enjoy gourmet dinners in vintage dining cars, or sightseeing through
the Cape Cod landscape. The railroad
teams up with Hy-Line Cruises for rail-
sail trips to the Kennedy compound.

Why Red?

Well, all of Toad's cars were red. So that's why mine are too.

DON'T FORGET TO BUY SOUVENIRS!

TVR

TREVOR'S CARS

TOAD HALL

MINI 73

**Toad Hall Classic Sports Car Museum**
HYANNIS

Toad, the Lord of Toad Hall (*Wind in the Willows*), loved red motorcars. So does Bill Putman, the owner of the Simmons Homestead Inn, in Hyannis Port. His private collection of more than 50 red classic cars is open for public viewing for a small admission.

**St. Francis Xavier Church** *(above and left)*
HYANNIS

White columns, arches, salmon-pink walls, and inspired stained glass art define the beautiful Roman Catholic sanctuary in Hyannis where the Kennedy clan worshipped and married, and where John F. Kennedy was an altar boy.

**Old Time Carousel** *(top)*

HYANNIS

The Cape Cod Carousel & Fun House Arcade in downtown Hyannis is a popular family tradition for vacationers. Naturally, there's ice cream and cotton candy, as well as kiddie rides and miniature golf.

**Cape Cod Potato Chips** *(bottom)*

HYANNIS

A whopping 250,000 people a year make the pilgrimage to the factory where the legendary kettle-cooked Cape Cod Potato Chips, as well as popcorn, tortilla chips, and salsa, are made. Tours are free and everyone gets to taste.

**Shopping Yarmouth** *(top)*
WEST YARMOUTH

Shopping, shopping, and more shopping are just three reasons to visit the charming Cape Cod village of West Yarmouth. The Antiques Center of Yarmouth has more than 100 vendors, and nearby is the charming thatch-roofed home of the famous Christmas Tree Shop.

**Edward Gorey House** *(bottom)*
YARMOUTH

Among the oldest houses in Yarmouth is the home of Edward Gorey (1925-2000), the eccentric author, artist, playwright, set designer, and animal rights activist. The home-turned-museum celebrates period architecture as well as Gorey's creative genius.

**Captain Bangs Hallet House**

YARMOUTH

Most of the original sea captains' homes throughout Cape Cod, dating back to the 1800s, are privately owned, so this one offers a rare glimpse into the lifestyle of the wealthy mariners. The museum houses treasures from China, maritime art and artifacts, and more.

**Judah Baker Windmill** *(top and opposite)*
YARMOUTH

Judah Baker's windmill, circa 1791, withstood more than two centuries of weather, nearly a century of milling grain, and the indignity of several moves from village to village. Now restored, it resides prettily at the public Windmill Park on the Bass River in Yarmouth.

**Black-eyed Susans** *(bottom)*
CAPE COD

A summertime rite of passage is the flashy display of black-eyed susans, like this one in Hyannis, that occur all over Cape Cod and the islands.

Judah Baker Windmill
Built 1791 Restored 1974 1999

## Swan Pond

DENNIS

Adirondack chairs in gardens and at water's edge are a common sight throughout Cape Cod, Martha's Vineyard, and Nantucket. Their pretty colors make an artful foreground for the summery blues and greens of Swan Pond, an authentic Cape Cod kettle pond.

**Timeless Beauty** (*above*)

DENNIS

In many places, the serenity of Cape Cod's marsh-fringed waterways seems little changed in hundreds of years. One might imagine a Wampanoag dugout canoe gliding silently along a canoe trail, with only the scream of a circling hawk to break the silence.

**Night on Bass River** (*pages 72–73*)

DENNIS

In the pre-dawn stillness, before Cape Cod awakes, there's barely a ripple in the water, and even the birds have not begun to think about breakfast. In a few hours the scene will be transformed like a theater set, bustling with recreational and commercial fishing activity.

**Herring River** *(top)*
DENNIS

A single red boat on a vast watery land-scape inspires the artist's imagination. Equally inspiring is the Herring River's rich history of cranberry farms, herring and alewife (shad) fisheries. Due to the threatened population, herring runs have been closed on Cape Cod in recent years.

**Howes Beach** *(bottom)*
DENNIS

Pristine white sands and gentle dunes make the Dennis coastline a choice spot for family photos and beach weddings. Favorable winds draw kiteboarders to Dennis, particularly to Howe's Beach and West Dennis Beach. Chapin Beach is among the most beautiful in the world.

**Magical Sunset**

DENNIS

No matter where you're headed at the sunset hour, sometimes you'll just have to be a few minutes late, as happened one magic evening somewhere along the Bass River in Dennis. Fortunately, there are plenty of perfect spots along the roadsides to pull off and gawk in safety.

**Rich Heritage** *(opposite)*
DENNIS

The culture and heritage of Cape Cod is expressed from the architecture of the museum building itself to the interactive presentations, permanent and traveling exhibitions, lectures, artist programs, classes, and field trips.

**Cape Cod Museum of Art** *(above and left)*
DENNIS

A majestic eagle with an eight-foot wingspan welcomes visitors to the Cape Cod Museum of art in Dennis, where more than 1,800 works of art celebrate local and regional talent. The eagle is part of the Birds of Steel series by Cape Cod artist Del Filardi.

**Flowering Fruit Trees** *(top)*
HARWICH

Among Cape Cod's showiest heralds of springtime is the awe-inspiring flowering cherry tree on the lawn of the Christian Science Church of Harwich. Throughout the Cape, springtime reveals her soft side with a profusion of flowering cherry, apple, and peach trees.

**Harwich Beach Dunes** *(bottom)*
HARWICH

Barely a ripple mars the perfect stillness of a cloudless spring afternoon along Highway 6, where a lone pine tree stands watch over the Harwich Beach dunes.

**Protected Coves** *(top)*

HARWICH

Those marvelous winds that make Cape Cod a world sailing center also can turn into the powerful gales and nor'easters that give Cape Cod its character. But there is no shortage of peaceful harbors and sheltered coves like the one in Harwichport.

**Wychmere Harbor** *(bottom)*

HARWICHPORT

One of the prettiest harbors in all of New England is Wychmere, ringed with grand homes, country clubs, and a marina; where a typical summer day will host more than 100 pleasure boats, private cruise and deep-sea fishing charter boats.

**Cape-Style Stores** *(opposite, top and bottom)*
HARWICH

With more than 20 beaches in Harwich alone, there's quite a demand for supplies, and the Town Center of Harwich offers it all in quaint and charming style. There also are galleries and boutiques, including the popular Adventures in Knitting, Cape Cod's oldest yarn shop.

**50 Golf Courses** *(above)*
HARWICHPORT

Cape Cod and the islands, with their dramatic seaside links and distinctive inland courses, rank among the top golf destinations in the country. Some, like the Harwichport Golf Course pictured here, have been designed as integral parts of historic villages.

**Springtime on the Cape** *(above and left)*
CHATHAM

It's showtime in April and May for the tulip, daffodil, burning bush, and a variety of dogwood and fruit trees. One event not to miss is Daffodil Days at Falmouth's Spohr Gardens.

**Atwood House Museum**

CHATHAM

Captain Atwood's 1752 home and many of its period furnishings have been faithfully maintained by the Chatham Historical Society. On the grounds is a re-created 1940s fishing camp. The light from the old Chatham lighthouse flashes during museum hours.

**Chatham Lighthouse** *(above and left)*

CHATHAM

Old sailors still whisper of ghostly horsemen swinging their lanterns on moonless, stormy nights, luring mariners to their doom. Some called them moon cussers. Whether due to ghosts, cussers or nature, the Chatham Lighthouse itself has twice succumbed to brutal storms. After the Chatham Light received state-of-the-art aerobeacons, its beautiful Fresnel lens was acquired by the Atwood House Museum.

**Cape Cod Style**

CHATHAM

Cedar shake siding, gables, balconies, wide verandahs, and pretty white fences were favored features of homes built in Chatham during the 18th and 19th centuries. Some of the thick hedge walls have been tended for more than a century.

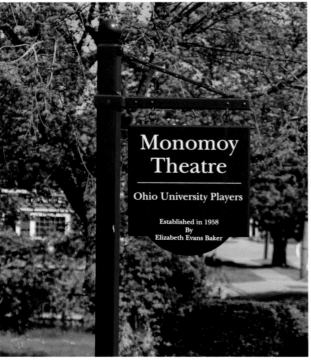

**Art and Candy** *(above)*

CHATHAM

Artistic hand-carved signs—and often the fragrance of homemade candy or pastries—entice customers into the locally owned sweet shops that are interspersed with fine galleries and boutiques on Chatham's Main Street.

**Monomoy Theatre** *(left)*

CHATHAM

Every summer for 50 years, members of the critically acclaimed Ohio University Players have commuted to their 1930s era theater in Chatham, where they perform to sold-out audiences with productions that range from Broadway musicals to Shakespeare.

**Chatham Railroad Museum** *(above)*
CHATHAM

Fish were its first passengers, and salt exports were the first freight when the railroad opened in 1887. Later, vacationers flocked to the colorful Victorian gothic depot. Retired in 1937, the old depot has been a museum since 1960.

**Red Caboose** *(right)*
CHATHAM

Restored to its 1910 perfection, the little red caboose that logged more than a million miles in the New York Central System now delights railroad buffs and children in Chatham.

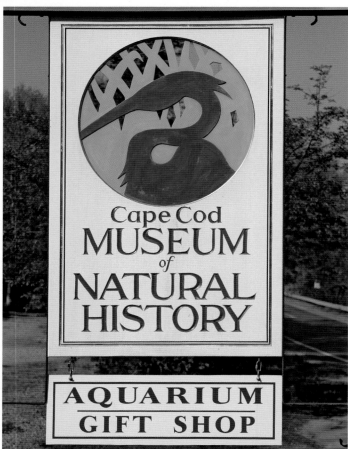

**Museum of Natural History** *(above and left)*
BREWSTER

Abutted by three hundred acres of conservation land, this 80-acre site is nature at her best. There are honeybee hives, an aquarium, and even a live osprey cam. The museum has an active calendar of lectures and events, including the popular Wednesday Walks around the Cape.

**Brewster Ladies Library** (*above and right*)
BREWSTER

Back in 1852, when it was started by twelve ladies from the town, male borrowers were required to pay a bit more than the ladies. The free community library still is a private institution maintained by The Brewster Ladies Library Association.

**Brewster Flats**

BREWSTER

Powerful receding tides on Cape Cod
Bay expose over a mile of ocean floor.
The resulting landscape, called the
Brewster Flats, is said to be the widest
expanse of tidal flats in North America.
Crabs, clams, and other mollusks remain
temporarily stranded in the tidal pools.

**Dip Me in the Water** *(top)*
BREWSTER

A cool dip in the ocean is a perfect way to finish a long bike ride along unspoiled marshlands and quiet beaches. For those who don't bring their own, there are more than 50 places to rent bikes throughout the Cape, Martha's Vineyard, and Nantucket.

**Oyster Farming** *(bottom)*
BREWSTER

Cape Cod is famous for its succulent oysters, and the Dennis Oyster, grown at the farm of John and Stephanie Lowell on Quivet Creek, was crowned the favorite at the Cape Cod Oyster Festival. The oyster farm is tended when specially-made gear is exposed at low tide.

91

**High Tide** *(top)*
BREWSTER

When visiting one of Brewster's ocean-
side beaches, the decision must be
whether one wants to walk or swim.
Those who would rather play in the surf
than explore the tidal pools should plan
their arrival near high tide.

**Sand Bars Exposed** *(bottom)*
WEST BREWSTER

Shimmery white tips of sandbars begin
to appear as the tide recedes on Brewster
beaches. All seven beaches have conven-
ient parking. Swimmers find the water
on the bay side to be warmer and calmer
than on the ocean side.

**Paine's Creek** *(top)*
BREWSTER

While several of the beaches, especially Crosby's Beach, are ideal for long walks at surf's edge, those seeking a spot away from foot traffic to park a beach chaise may prefer Paine's Creek Beach.

**Ripples in the Sand** *(bottom)*
BREWSTER

At low tide, marsh grasses and tidal markings are exposed, transforming the sand into an artist's canvas of golden ripples, marked only with the footprints of sea birds searching for their breakfast.

**Golden Sunrise**

ORLEANS

Dawn breaks like a golden curtain rising
on the little fleet of vessels at rest in
Town Cove. The sheltered cove lies at
the end of Nauset Marsh in Orleans.

**Jonathan Young Mill** *(top)*
ORLEANS

Adjacent to Town Cove is a picturesque windmill built more than two and a half centuries ago. Though retired from its job of milling corn, its works still function, and guides are on hand for tours.

**Uncle Seth's Pond** *(bottom)*
ORLEANS

The family-friendly warm water pond with the sandy bottom is as cozy as its name. Peaceful and fringed with a grassy lawn, the little Orleans beach is especially popular with families.

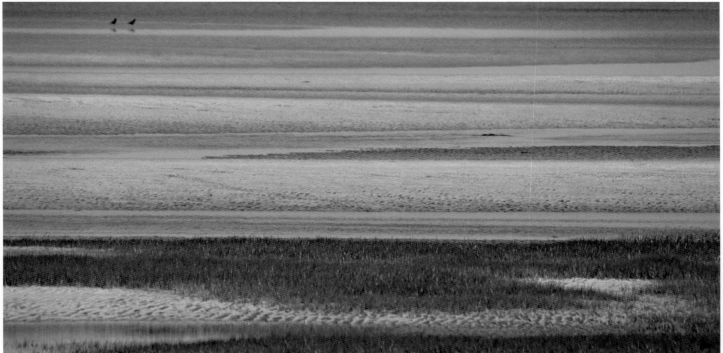

**Gentle Slopes** *(top and bottom)*

ORLEANS

Nauset Beach (top) and Skaket Beach
(bottom) are gently sloped white sand
beaches. With a nine-foot tidal change,
a dramatic transformation takes place at
low tide. Bits of seaweed and shells are
often caught in lush sea grasses, which
are fully submerged during high tide.

**The Sisters** *(top)*

EASTHAM

Once there were three demure ladies in white dresses and black hats. The 15-foot lighthouses, dubbed the Three Sisters of Nauset, distinguished Eastham from North Truro and Chatham. The red and white Nauset Light was brought from Chatham to represent the Three Sisters.

**Coast Guard Beach** *(bottom)*

EASTHAM

The forty-mile stretch of beach that Henry David Thoreau named the great Outer Beach starts at the tip of Nauset Spit, just south of the former Coast Guard surf-rescue station. It is now managed by the National Park Service and is considered one of the best beaches in the U.S.

## Picture Window

EASTHAM

The Eastham Visitor Center on the Cape Cod National Seashore has excellent interpretive programs, a fine museum, and a bookstore. One of its most compelling attractions is the spectacular panoramic view of marsh, pond, beach, ocean, and sky.

**Sunrises and Sunsets** *(top)*

EASTHAM

The first and last hour of each day brings a different light and a different mood. At first light, it may be the promise of a great day's catch. As the setting sun turns the world golden, it's the feeling—for at least a moment—that all's right with the world.

**Wooden Boat Magic** *(bottom)*

EASTHAM

Wooden boat enthusiasts keep sharp eyes out for visual treasures on canals and ponds of Cape Cod, Martha's Vineyard, and Nantucket. Occasionally, one is rewarded with a chance encounter like the perfect red specimen spotted early one morning on Collins Pond.

## Nauset Light Beach

EASTHAM

A solitary lifeguard stand emphasizes
the vastness of the beach and dunes at
Nauset Beach, on one of America's most
spectacular coastlines. Strong receding
tides in winter often expose the remains
of one of the Three Sisters lights.

### Alone in a Crowd

EASTHAM

The breathtaking scale of Nauset Beach makes it nearly impossible to appear crowded, even on a summer Sunday morning. The beach stretches for ten miles to Orleans, with special sections reserved for permitted off-road vehicles.

**Bird Watching** *(top)*
WELLFLEET

The Outer Cape, which begins in Orleans
and encompasses Eastham, Wellfleet,
Truro, and Provincetown, shelters a
diverse population of songbirds and
shore birds. Birders can follow self-
guided trails or join naturalist walks from
the Wellfleet Bay Wildlife Sanctuary.

**Wildlife Sanctuary** *(bottom)*
WELLFLEET

The Audubon-managed Wellfleet Bay
Wildlife Sanctuary is set on 1,100 acres
of marshes, woodlands, and ponds. It
includes hummingbird and butterfly gardens, and offers naturalist-guided marine
life cruises and excursions to Monomoy
National Wildlife Reserve in Chatham.

**Breakers** *(top)*

WELLFLEET

Rolling waves on LeCount Hollow Beach bring to mind a quote from Henry Beston's book, *The Outermost House*: "The volutes of the breakers approach, tumble, and dissolve, and over the glisten, the foam, and moist, sea-fragrant air still fly the small shorebirds hastening."

**Mini-Vacation** *(bottom)*

WELLFLEET

The sand of LeCount Hollow Beach is close to the road, making a quick lunchtime beach escape easy for locals. Families with small children enjoy the shallow, wider than average tidal pools, which are several degrees warmer than the ocean.

**Sunrise** *(top)*
WELLFLEET

In the ephemeral moments between the
first hint of dawn and the promise of a
gorgeous summer day, both sea and sky
are bathed in light, infused with lavender, red, and gold. A sailor's forecast
states, *"Red sky in the morning, sailors take
warning. Red sky at night, sailors delight."*

**Parabolic Dunes** *(bottom)*
WELLFLEET

Sand dunes make ideal hosts for hardy
vegetation that thrives on salty winds
and dry soil. In return, dune grass and
other plants such as chokecherry, bear-
berry, beach heather, and lichen serve
as anchors to protect the dunes from
erosion and wind destruction.

**Cahoon Hollow Beach**
WELLFLEET

A sandy path fringed in sea grasses and flowers meanders down the massive dunes to the Cahoon Hollow Beach, where there are neither stairs nor signs, or any other obstructions to mar the natural views of sea and sand.

**Outermost Cottages**

WELLFLEET

No phone, televison, or internet are among key selling points of the Cook family's 14 dune-top cottages. Those wishing to experience the Cape Cod of Henry Beston's , *The Outermoust House*, will find the ambience almost unchanged since its writing more than 80 years ago.

**The Lobster Man** *(top)*
WELLFLEET

Repeat visitors to the National Seashore eagerly watch for their first glimpse of the famous lobsterman, built atop a restaurant in Wellfleet. The building may change names but the hardy lobsterman has remained for years.

**No Child Left Inside** *(bottom)*
WELLFLEET

The National Park Service maintains the Cape Cod National Seashore, with an extensive calendar of guided walks and talks, interactive exhibits and fascinating children's programs such as the outdoor adventure, "No Child Left Inside."

**Wellfleet Harbor Actor's Theater** *(top)*
WELLFLEET

*WHAT* earned critical acclaim for more than 20 years with only a glued-together former nightclub. It recently christened the Julie Harris Stage, a state-of-the-art, 200-seat venue to showcase its cutting-edge theater productions. The theater is located at 2357 Route 6.

**Slice of Americana** *(bottom)*
WELLFLEET

The more things change, the more they stay the same. Young lemonade vendors take advantage of the summer traffic along Main Street in Wellfleet to earn spending money for themselves and extra for a worthy cause. So please, don't forget the tip.

**Reflect on This** *(opposite)*
WELLFLEET

This Wellfleet scene showcases all the elements of the quintessential Cape Cod neighborhood, right down to the walking bridge and the church tower.

**Hatch's Fish & Produce Market** (*top*)
WELLFLEET

Young Cliff Hatch started his business half a century ago selling fresh fish door to door from his pickup truck. Today, people wait in line when the fish comes off the boats. Hatch's also carries organic produce, cut flowers, and homemade honey and jams from area farms.

**Wellfleet Flea Market** (*bottom*)
WELLFLEET

Treasure hunters descend on the Wellfleet Drive-in-Theater every weekend, to sort through the bounty of as many as 300 sellers during the high season. Antiques, garage sale items, housewares, crafts, and probably the kitchen sink, are waiting to be bargained for.

**Cape Cod Souvenirs**

WELLFLEET

Beach-goers lacking their buckets and shovels can find all they need at this roadside shop. Pick up a starfish float, sunscreen, and some salt water taffy for a snack… and stop on your way home for just the right souvenir.

**Truro Vineyard**

TRURO

Vineyard and winery tours and tastings
add a heady flavor to the Cape Cod
experience at the Roberts family vineyard. The Truro Vineyard produces nine
maritime wines on a former 1830s era
farm. There's a lovely gift shop in the
restored 19th century Federal house.

## Cape Cod Light

TRURO

Henry David Thoreau slept in this Truro lighthouse, which had the first flashing light in the United States. Originally called Highland Light, it overlooks one of the largest graveyards of wrecked ships on the Cape. In his book, *Cape Cod,* Thoreau wrote: "[to] feel the full force of a tempest; take up your residence on the top of Mount Washington, or at the Highland Light."

**Longnook Beach**

TRURO

The colorful beach umbrellas, crowds of swimmers and sunbathers, and even the rolling surf are dwarfed by the sheer magnitude of the dunes at Longnook Beach. Those seeking solitude and miles of unspoiled nature need only step a few yards away from the nearest parking lot.

114

## Going Barefoot

TRURO

Apparently it's easier to walk barefoot in the soft sand at the base of massive sand dunes, if masses of abandoned footwear give any clue. Soaring more than 100 feet over the tide line, the dunes at Truro are the highest on Cape Cod.

**View from the Monument** (*top and bottom*)
PROVINCETOWN

The Pilgrim Monument yields some of the most spectacular views in New England. In Provincetown Harbor, fishing trawlers and sightseeing boats add dimension to the view of pleasure boats along the docks. The natural harbor is a mile long and three miles wide.

**Pilgrim Monument** (*opposite*)
PROVINCETOWN

Many people are unaware that the Mayflower landed first in Provincetown Harbor. It is where the Mayflower Contract was drawn up and the first child born to Pilgrims in New England was born here. The Traditional Lighting of the Monument ceremony on

Thanksgiving Day involves approximately 3,500 lights, which remain illuminated through New Year's Day.

**Artful Ascent**

PROVINCETOWN

In 1907, President Theodore Roosevelt sailed to Provincetown on the presidential yacht, *Mayflower*, to lay the cornerstone of the Pilgrim Monument. There are 60 ramps and 116 steps to the top of the nearly 253-foot monument, which is the tallest granite structure in America.

**Town Crier Bells and More** *(top and bottom)*
PROVINCETOWN

From the bells and attire of town criers, to artifacts and replications of the *Mayflower*, the Provincetown Museum brings history to life. Its collection even includes the town's first fire engine, built by an apprentice of Paul Revere. While the primary focus is on the *Mayflower* pilgrims and Provincetown history, the ever-changing exhibitions keep the museum experience fresh. The museum and monument together, locally called PMPM (Pilgrim Monument and Provincetown Museum) are on High Pole Hill Road overlooking the town center.

### Whydah Museum
PROVINCETOWN

The *Whydah Gally*, wrecked in a 1717 nor'easter off the coast of Cape Cod, was a pirate ship under the command of the dastardly Black Sam Bellamy. The first authenticated pirate wreck ever found, its salvage operation by The National Geographic Society has been in progress for two decades. Interactive displays, weaponry, ship models, and pieces of eight are among the museum treasures.

## PAAM
PROVINCETOWN

*Reclining Nude* by Penelope Jencks welcomes guests to the Provincetown Art Association and Museum. The museum houses historic and contemporary permanent collections, and hosts world class traveling exhibitions, concerts, and art classes.

**Nice Buoys** *(top)*
PROVINCETOWN

To lobstermen, a buoy is like a personal fingerprint. Distinctive patterns of bars and hues make it easy to identify traps. After a storm, dislodged buoys make bright finds for beachcombers. The colorful buoy wall at Townsend Lobster Co. is a popular Provincetown landmark.

**Chariots for Hire** *(bottom)*
PROVINCETOWN

Locals book their PediCab chariots months in advance for the outrageous and colorful annual Provincetown carnival. PediCab rides add to the ambience of Provincetown for visitors by offering a variety of specialty tours from galleries to graveyards.

## Commercial Street

PROVINCETOWN

The rainbow-hued main street of Provincetown is one of the happiest spots on the Cape. Fine art, jewelry, antique, and clothing boutiques rub shoulders on Commercial Street with lively cabarets, quirky kitsch emporiums, and quaint B&Bs.

## On The Water

PROVINCETOWN

Beachy summer rental cottages and seaside restaurants dominate the picture-postcard view of Provincetown Harbor from the MacMillan Pier. The pier is the center of lively activity, from whale tours to commercial fishing to colorful processions and the annual Pier Dance.

**Dune Shacks** *(top)*
PROVINCETOWN

Scattered atop isolated grassy dunes in the Provincelands are 19 artful shanties; all that remain of a1920s-era writers' colony. Built in the 1800s to shelter shipwreck rescue crews, the shacks became retreats for literary giants cummings, Kerouac, Mailer, O'Neill and others.

**Flying In** *(bottom)*
PROVINCETOWN

The single runway at Provincetown Municipal Airport stays busy with more than 250 general aviation flights a day, along with the year-round operations of its one commercial airline, Cape Air.

**Pilgrim Lake** *(top)*
PROVINCETOWN

Pilgrim Lake, or as it is historically known, East Harbor, is one of Cape Cod's original inner harbors. The stark, wind-swept dunes that rise right out of the water afford breathtaking views.

**Rooftop in the Dunes** *(bottom)*
PROVINCETOWN

The massive scale of the Provincetown dunes is evidenced by the dwarfed rooftop of a large home tucked into the treeline. The Cape Cod National Seashore encompasses more than 43,000 acres and thirty-plus miles of unbroken shoreline.

**Grand Entrance**

PROVINCETOWN

The expansive blue waters of Pilgrim
Lake on the approach from Truro to
Provincetown invoke a breathtaking
sensation of being embraced by the sea.

**Wisteria as Art** *(top)*
PROVINCETOWN

Residents of Cape Cod, Martha's Vineyard, and Nantucket are famous for their dedication to their cottages and their gardens. This stunning display of wisteria and matching shutters begs the question: will the paint colors change with the gardening season?

**Secret Lanes** *(bottom)*
PROVINCETOWN

Charming cottages and landscapes are tucked cozily along narrow, unpaved lanes. Here in this magical place where American history began, there's sure to be another discovery just around the next bend in the road.